Copyright

Mpdawn Publications

This edition written, printed and published by

Mpdawn publications 2016

D.A.Weaver

CW01497640

2

## FISH IDENTIFICATION

The Species of fish shown in this book are the main ones caught from or found in the water ways throughout the United Kingdom.

Some species of fish are more plentiful than others, and many of these tend to look similar in size, shape and colour with many of these having the same fin and tail configuration.

The habitat in which these fish live, swim and feed can greatly affect the colourations and markings on different species of fish, this should always be taken into account when identifying a species.

Always be aware that on game fish there may be a size limit in force, depending on which river or lake you happen to be fishing.

Fish that are to be returned to the water must be handled carefully, it is always better to handle them with either wet hands or a damp towel, as this will prevent causing any damage to the fish scales, fins, eyes and rest of body.

When returning a fish to the water it is always best to carry it down to the edge and not drop it from a great height, the fish should be given time to recover from the ordeal of being landed before you let it return, unharmed to the water, in most cases it is best to keep the fish in a submerged net during this period and if a net is not available support the fishes body and hold the base of the tail until the fish tries to swim away.

## FISH IDENTIFICATION DIAGRAM

The diagram below is for the angler to examine so that he or she should be able to determine the correct name of fins e.t.c, and in doing so help towards the identification of various species of fish, however if in doubt, ask your local tackle dealer as he or she should be able to help with any identification marks that may have been missed by the angler.

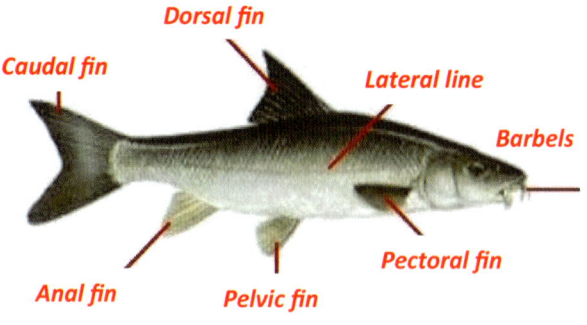

*Dorsal fin*

*Caudal fin*

*Lateral line*

*Barbels*

*Anal fin*

*Pelvic fin*

*Pectoral fin*

4

The fish that are covered in this book are the main species that are fished for around the United Kingdom by the coarse angler, please note that species such as stickle backs etc. are only briefly mentioned, however the limited shell fish, and game fish are at the rear of the book.

Please also note that a current Environment Agency rod fishing licence is required by law to fish on the waterways of England, although there a number of concessions in place for the junior, the disabled and the older members of the population.

Fishing for Game fish such as salmon and trout etc. requires a game fishing license, please read the Game fishing introduction towards the rear of the book.

### *Environment Agency rod fishing licence:*

### *Who needs a licence?*

Anyone aged 12 years or over who fishes for salmon, trout, freshwater fish or eels in England, Wales or the

Border Esk in Scotland, must have an Environment Agency rod fishing licence.

### *Who qualifies for a concessionary licence?*

You are eligible for a concessionary licence if:

You are aged 12 to 16 inclusive (Junior)

You are aged 65 years or over (Senior)

You have a Blue Badge parking concession, or are in receipt of Disability Living Allowance any rate.

### *What counts as proof of eligibility?*

Anglers aged 65 or over will need to provide one of the following:

Birth certificate, Drivers licence, Valid passport, Medical card.

Eligible disabled anglers will need to show either their blue badge or a recent letter from the Department of Work and Pensions showing their receipt of Disability Living Allowance (PIPS).

The statutory coarse fish close season applies between

15 March and 15 June (inclusive). It applies on all rivers, streams and drains in England and Wales, and to some canals and some still waters around the United Kingdom, the species in this book are found in the areas marked in red on the map below and although these fish are also found in the republic of Ireland, this area does not fall under the United Kingdom's derestriction.

### *Barbus barbus*

These fish have elongated bodies and are flat bellied, the shape of the head is almost pointed and scale free and the eyes are rather small and are set high on the sides of the head, the lips are quite thick with two pairs of fleshy barbels. The dorsal fin of the Barbel is quite high and has a strong spine at the leading edge of the fin, the anal fin is short based and rounded. The body is covered with fairly small scales that are firmly embedded in skin, there are approximately 60 scales in the formation of the lateral line. The strong broad tail and torpedo shaped body gives this fish the ability to take off at a great rate of knots whilst still hugging to the riverbed. Colouration is a warm greeny brown on the back, golden yellow on the sides and ventrally, the fins are fairly dark except for the pectoral, pelvic and anal fins which are a yellowish orange. This species has been caught up to weights of 21.1 lbs.

**Barbel:**

*Rhodeus sericeus*

*Bitterling:*

This is a deep bodied and moderately compressed fish, with the back arched anterior to the dorsal fin. The scales of this mini species are moderately large for the fishes overall size. Colouration across the back is a greyish green to greyish brown, and the sides and belly are silvery, however the sides may also include some pink and slight gold tints.

The fins are pale orange, but also quite clear, except in breeding males when the dorsal and anal fins become bright red.

A greyish green metallic stripe runs along the mid line of the body from just under the dorsal fin to the caudal peduncle. This small species has been caught up to 12 drams in weight.

### *Alburnus alburnas*

Bleak are slim bodied fish, with an almost pointed scale free head, the mouth is oblique opening on the upper surface of the head, the eyes of this small fish are quite large in comparison to the rest of the head.

Colouration of the bleak is generally a shiny silvery colour, however, the back and flanks of the fish are a silvery bluish green, merging into silver down the sides to a white belly. The main body of the fish is covered with large scales care should be taken when handling this species as these scales are loose and very easily dislodged.

The lateral line is complete and the fins are pointed, these are colourless, this species has a long anal fin that is concave at the edge and the tail fin (caudal) is deeply forked.

This fish has been caught up to 4oz 9drams.

**Bleak:**

*Abramis Brama*

**Bream:**

Bream are deep bodied fish with flat sides and a high back, young specimens tend to be more slender.

The head of this species is relatively small and scale free with small eyes, the mouth can extend ventrally to form a tube, this is primarily used when feeding.

The body scales are quite small, approximately 55 of these make up the lateral line.

The anal fin is strongly concave, the fins of the fish are a greyish brown, ventrally tinted with red.

Colouration of the main body of the fish is dark brown or greyish bronze on the back with the sides being a golden brown, the fins can be almost black in colour, juvenile fish tend to be silvery sided.

11

### *Blicca Bjoerkna*

Silver Bream are a fairly deep bodied fish with a high back, the eyes are moderately larger than the common variety of Bream and the head is small and scale free, the dorsal is quite high and measures almost one third of the body depth. The body scales of this species are quite large and approximately 46 of these make up the lateral line. Colouration of the main body of the fish is a light olive brown on the back with the sides being a brilliant silver, not to be mistaken for a juvenile Common Bream. The fins of the fish are a dusky greyish brown except for the pectoral and pelvic fins which are orange with grey tips.

Much smaller than the common variety this species grows up to 2lb.2oz.

### *Silver Bream:*

# *Carp (General)*

Carp are one of the most adaptable species in the United Kingdom, after it's introduction in the 13th century one or another member of the species are found in most ponds, lakes, canals, rivers and some chalk streams, in fact the carp species tend to thrive in almost any fresh water environment. Initially introduced to the United Kingdom by monks for use as a food source, this species has captured the hearts and minds of many anglers and since the first recorded 40lb fish in the early 1950s the sport and variety have both increased. The record now stands at over 66lbs and although fish of this size are very rare, fish in the 10lbs to 30lbs are becoming more common with specimen fish being held in many private waters.

**The different variants of carp are as follows:**

**Common carp**.

These are fully scaled, baring the head.

**Crucian.**

These are similar to the common carp but much smaller and no barbules.

**Mirror carp.**

These have large, uneven mirror like scales and where these are absent the body is smooth.

**Linear carp.**

These are scale less except for a row of large scales that run along the lateral line on both sides of the fish.

**Leather carp.**

These are smooth bodied, except occasionally near the dorsal fin.

**Grass carp.**

These are similar to the common carp but normally have a longer, thinner body.

**Ghost carp.**

These are the same as the common carp however it is all white with two black eyes.

**Koi carp.**

These are similar to the common but with colours that include orange, black, red, yellow, white and a combination of these colours.

*Cyprinus carpio*

**Common Carp:**

The Common Carp has a scaled body and yet the head is scale free, the dorsal fin is long based with it's free edge being concave, there is a stout spine with serrated rear edges, the carp is toothless but they do have two barbels at each side of the mouth one on each side being longer. Colouration of the common carp is brown to greenish brown or golden brown with a lighter brown, cream underside. Caught up to 56lbs 6oz. Carp are found in all waters, but are fished for predominantly in still waters. The carp feed extensively on bottom living invertebrates, fresh water shrimp, snails, insect larvae, caddis larvae, nymphs, crustaceans and molluscs, grubbing around among the bottom debris for the many micro-organisms which live there. Should the need arise this species will also consume water plants and small fish fry.

### *Cyprinus carpio*

Ghost Carp (Cyprinus carpio) is a variation of Common Carp brought about by extensive hybridization between different populations of the common carp. Scientific consensus is that there are at least two subspecies of the common carp, one from Western Eurasia and another from East Asia these are (Cyprinus carpio carpio) and (Cyprinus carpio haematopterus). Human interference and highly selective breeding over many years have produced many varieties from these two strains of common carp. The variations in colour and pattern, in both fully scaled and partially scaled fish, is considerable with many clearly identifiable patterns having been bred and named. There are a great number of colour variations within Ghost Carp ranging from bright white to gunmetal grey and their colours can and do develop as they age. This variant has been caught up to 41 lbs.

**Ghost Carp:**

*Carassius carassius*

**Crucian Carp:**

The Crucian Carp is amongst the smallest members of the family, which includes other fish such as the Common Carp. Although this species is of the same family as the Common Carp, the Crucian Carp is different as it doesn't have barbules and rarely reaches a weight above 3.5lb, however U.K. record stands just over 4lb 9oz.

Crucian Carp vary in colour from gold to bronze but mainly have a brownish colouring across the back with gold or greyish green sides leading down to a yellowish or white belly. The body of the fish is normally rounded and has a covering of small scales in an even pattern. The fins of the Crucian are rounded whilst the dorsal fin is convex, colouration of the fins is usually reddish.

## *Ctenopharyngodon idella*

This species of carp has been introduced to many countries around the world with the United kingdom being just one in a very long list. Grass carp have an elongated, torpedo shaped body. The mouth is slightly oblique with non fleshy, firm lips, note the lack of barbels. The lateral line contains 40 to 42 scales. The dorsal fin has eight to ten soft rays, and the anal fin is set closer to the tail than most other cyprinids. Colouration is dark bronzy brown across the back and has deep golden coloured sides blending in to a creamy white under belly, the fins of this fish tend to be large and brown, the scales of this fish tend to be quite large and slightly outlined with a dark edge. This member of the species has been caught up to 48lbs in weight around the United kingdom, however the maximum recorded weight worldwide is 88lbs and at a length of 4.6 feet this was truly a monster of a fish.

*Grass Carp:*

*Cyprinus Carpio*

*Koi Carp:*

Koi or more specifically nishikigoi, literally meaning "brocaded carp" are ornamental varieties of the domesticated common carp (Cyprinus carpio) that are kept for decorative purposes in outdoor koi ponds, lakes or water gardens.

Koi varieties are distinguished by coloration, patterning, and scalation. The word koi comes from Japanese, simply meaning "carp." It includes both the dull grey fish and the brightly coloured varieties.

Some of the major colours are white, black, red, yellow, blue, and cream. The most popular category of koi is the Gosanke, which is made up of the Kohaku, Taisho Sanshoku, and Showa Sanshoku varieties.

Although originally bread for food this particular member of the carp family are now highly prized fish.

19

*Cyprinus Carpio*

**Leather Carp:**

A true leather Carp has no scales on its body at all although it is accepted that a fish with line of scales underneath the dorsal fin is still counted a Leather Carp.

The body colour of the fish can range from a pale yellow to a dark gold colour and slightly lighter on the belly, the leather carp is another variation of the common carp as are the mirror and ghost, this one is said to have been bread by monks to have fewer scales to aid the preparation and cleaning of the fish before cooking. Contrary to popular belief, Leather carp are not Mirror carp without scales, there is a distinct genetic difference, Leather carp also have a reduced number of red blood cells, slowing growth rates, this species can still grow in excess of 54lbs and although it is small when put up against the world record mirror carp, this is still a big fish.

### *Cyprinus Carpio*

The Mirror carp has a more rounded shape to its body and tends to be more 'stocky' than the other varieties of common carp. The main body colouration can be dependent on the water conditions and can range from pale yellow to a dark gold, the scales on the body are generally huge and non uniform in pattern compared to the common carp however there are exceptions to the rule. Fish can be found with a linear line of scales down each side, these are linear mirror, and with a full set of large random scales all over the body, these are fully scaled.

Two Tone the 67 lb. 14oz. Mirror that held the united kingdom record was reported dead in 2010, this record still stands as a testament to a great fish. The mirror carps world record weight of 101 lb. 4oz is held by a fish in Hungary, caught and landed in June 2012.

*Mirror Carp:*

## Cyprinus Carpio

The wild carp is basically a wild version of the common carp, one of the main differences is the body tends to be elongated similar to the grass carp shape, however with this variety you notice that the dorsal fin is more like the common carps. There are two barbels each side of mouth, these are shorter on the top lip. Colouration of the wild carp is a brownish green on the back and upper sides, blending to golden yellow ventrally. The fins are dusky, ventrally with a reddish tinge. This variety can grow in excess of 25 lbs. The wild populations of this species are considered vulnerable to extinction, however the species has also been domesticated and introduced into environments worldwide, and is often considered a very destructive invasive species, and as a result has been included in the List of the world's 100 worst invasive species.

*Ameiurus melas*

The black bullhead is a species of bullhead catfish, like other bullhead catfish, it has the ability to thrive in waters that are low in oxygen, brackish, turbid and very warm. Like virtually all catfish, it is nocturnal, preferring to feed at night, although young will feed during the day. Colouration is usually black, dark olive, or dark brown across the back, their belly is greenish to creamy white or yellowish. They have dark chin barbels and lack mottled markings on their sides. Average sizes are between eight and fourteen inches and up to 1lbs, however specimens of these have been taken from the water over that weight. This species has spines at the base of the pectoral and dorsal fins, care should be taken when handling this species as although it is a relatively small fish the spines can cause wounds to go septic, these can also be quite painful.

### *Black Bullhead:*

*Silurus glanis*

*Wels Catfish:*

This species of catfish has a long, scale free body, with a large head and mouth the inside of which has hundreds of tiny little hooked like teeth on the top and bottom jaws, these are used to hold prey before passing it to the two sets of crushing pads at the back of the throat. The Wels catfish has six barbules, the two long ones on the upper jaw are for detecting its prey. It has a very small dorsal fin although the anal fin stretches almost to the tail. The colouration of the Wels can vary from fish to fish but normally they have dark eyes with a dark greeny black back, creamy yellowish sides creating a mottled effect and lighter under belly. These are caught up to and over 60 lb. however there has been reports and records of this species weight and length going back to the 19th century, some of these are listed at over 500 lb. and 13 ft. in length.

### *Leuciscus cephalus*

Chub are popular with anglers due to their readiness to feed, and thus to be caught, in almost any conditions. Small chub are freely biting fish which even the inexperienced anglers find easy to catch. As they become larger, however, chub become more wary and are easily spooked by noise or visual disturbance, as a consequence fish over the weight of 2kg are targeted. This species has a large head with a protruding upper lip, it has a large mouth and thick lips, care should be taken when removing hooks as these have sharp, bone crushing pharyngeal teeth at the back of their mouths. Colouration is simply dark grey brown along the back running into a brass colour along the sides. Both the dorsal fin and tail fin are dark grey, while the underside pelvic and anal fins are a shade of orange. These fish have been taken from the water with a weight in excess of 8 lbs.

*Chub:*

*Leuciscus leuciscus*

*Dace:*

Colouration of the Dace is a dusky blue across the head and back whilst the sides have a shining silvery aspect to them, with numerous dark lines running along the course of the scales. The ventral and anal fins are white, tinged with pale red, and the dorsal, pectoral and caudal fins are tipped with black. Although this is a small species, specimens of over 1 lbs. 4oz have been caught, with the record weight around the world of 2.2lb and a length of 15 inches. The common Dace live in fresh and brackish water and is at home in many of the rivers and streams around the United kingdom and Europe, it is a very lively and active fish, unfortunately It is preyed upon by the larger predaceous fishes of fresh waters, and owing to its silvery appearance is a favourite bait in pike angling. The dace feeds on worms, insects, insect-larvae, snails, and also vegetable matter when other food supplies are short.

*Anguilla Anguilla*

The European Eel has a long, snake like body, tiny eyes, tiny pectoral fins and a dorsal fin that begins a third of the way down the body and extends right back to the tip of the pointed tail and along the underside of the belly. The head of an eel is very streamlined and small, pointed with the mouth full of rows of tiny teeth. Unlike many other migrating fish, eels begin their lifecycle in the ocean and spend most of their lives in fresh water only returning to the ocean to spawn and then die. Colouration is a yellowish brown across the back and sides but lighter underneath this however changes to a metallic silvery bronze before the eel makes its long journey to the sea to breed. Specimens of over 10 lbs. have been taken from the water.

*Eel:*

27

*Leuciscus idus*

**Golden Orfe:**

The wild varieties of this species colouration is a greyish olive colour on the back and upper sides blending to silver on the lower sides and a silvery white on the belly, captive fish display a different colouration, closer to that of a goldfish these tend to be more orange across the back and shoulders, blending to a creamy white under belly. Both anal and pelvic fins are a reddish colour, while the tail and dorsal fin can be greyish. In older and bigger fish the body colour can turn to yellow bronze. The Golden Orfe also known as the Ide has been caught up to 8 lbs. 5ozs in the united kingdom, the Orfe/Ide can grow larger in other parts of the world and has been recorded at a weight of 9 lb. and 79cm in length. The golden Orfe/ide started its life as an ornamental pond fish stock in many parts of the world, over the years these have reached the wild via flood or with un-sanctioned help, now they can be found in many of the rivers and streams around the world.

### *Gobio gobio*

A slender bodied fish with a curved back, gudgeon have a flattened belly and a rather large head. The body is round in cross section, compressed towards the tail. Like the barbel the mouth is on the ventral surface of the head with a barbel at each corner, the lips are fairly thick for a fish of this size. The body has rather large scales with approximately 42 In the lateral line, the head is scale free. Both dorsal and anal fins are short.

Colouration is a greeny brown on the back, yellowish on the sides with a series of large dusky patches, Cream ventrally. Dorsal, tail and anal fins are heavily spotted, these fish are caught with a weight up to 5oz. The Gudgeon can be found schooling in quite large numbers in rivers, lakes and canals and can produce great sport when targeted on very light tackle.

**Gudgeon:**

29

*Phoxinus phoxinus*

*Minnow:*

Minnow is a general term used to refer to small freshwater and saltwater fish, especially those used as bait fish or for fishing bait. More specifically, it refers to small freshwater fish of the family cyprinidae, these are also known in Ireland as pinkeens. Minnow have variable colourations, according to the maturity stage, age and environment of the fish. Normally the back is brownish green, and is separated from the whitish grey ventral side by a longitudinal series of blotches that may unite into a dark line. Males are brightly coloured during the spawning season, with white spots on the fins, reddish pectoral and pelvic fins, black throat, greenish tinge along the sides, and a scarlet belly. This mini species has been caught up to 13.5 drams, however this is normally targeted by youngsters using a small fishing net and commonly kept in a small glass jar for the duration of the trip.

*Perca fluviatus*

The perch has long been a target for most junior anglers from first catching them in a small net to first hooking in to one on rod and line. The shape of the body varies but, mostly slender bodied with a short head, a rounded, blunt snout. Perch have two dorsal fins, the first with 13-15 long spines joined at the base to the second dorsal. The anal fin is short based with 2 sharp spines at the front. Pelvic fins are set close together, each with a spine in it. Teeth in the jaws are small but numerous. Colouration is striking with the back being a greeny-brown becoming green on the sides and creamy on the belly. There are a series of dark vertical bars running along the sides and a dark spot at the end of the dorsal fin, ventral fins are deep orange. These grow in excess of 5 lbs.

**Perch:**

*Esox Lucius*

## Pike:

The pike has a long, torpedo shaped body with dorsal and anal fins close to the tail. The head is pointed from the side view, with a flat snout. The lower jaws have several massive fangs and hundreds of small sharp teeth on the palate. Colouration is greenish brown across the back, the sides are greenish, flecked with golden lines and speckles, sometimes forming bars. Colour patterns are specific to the individual fish, just like a fingerprint, no two are the same. Pike grow to a relatively large size, however the average length is about 70 to 120 cm, even so, lengths of up to 150 cm and weights of 25 kg are very rare. The heaviest specimen known so far was caught in 1983 in Germany, this specimen was 147 cm long and weighed 31 kg. The longest pike ever recorded and confirmed was 152 cm long and weighed 28 kg. The United kingdom average weight is up to and just over 46 lbs.

### *Lepomis gibbosus*

This is a small and very colourful fish, averaging five to six inches in length, although some can grow to 10". The body is covered with translucent blue green irregular spots, whilst the head is marked with horizontal light fluorescent stripes with a red tipped gill cover, the under belly of this species is a yellowish orange colour. This species has been taken up to 14 oz. 5 drams. The unconfirmed world record for this fish stands at 1 lb. 6oz. In the United kingdom and the rest of Europe this fish is classed as an invasive species, out competing existing species for both food and territory, the pumpkinseed tend to feed best on bright late afternoons where they can be found schooling together.

### *Pumpkinseed:*

*Rutilus Rutilus*

*Roach:*

Roach are often confused with the Rudd and although these two fish are similar in shape and size, there are a number of differences that distinguish them apart, the eye colour, body colouration and fin colours.

This species is a silvery blue in colour across the back blending to a white under belly, this fish has fairly large scales, a deep body and forward facing mouth, fins are an orange red colour and there is a red tinge to the eye.

The lateral line is made up by approximately 45 scales. Juvenile specimens tend to have a more slender body where as older specimens get a higher and broader body shape.

This species has been taken up to 4lbs. 3oz in weight and up to a maximum length of 50cm.

34

### *Scardinius erythrophthalmus*

Rudd and roach appear similar, but the recognition of true Rudd is really quite simple. The mouth is angled steeply upwards and the leading edge of the dorsal fin is behind the base of the pelvic fins, also each eye has a deep yellow iris, with a red spot just above it. Colouration is a bluish green across the back which blends to a golden coloured flank and silvery white under belly, the fins are a deep orange colour and almost deep red when seen underwater. Another difference between the Rudd and Roach is the amount of rays in the dorsal fins, the Rudd has 8 to 9 where as the Roach has between 10 and 12 fin rays. This fish has been taken up to 4 lbs.10 oz. and up to a length of 45 to 50cm, however the average size is closer to 25cm and 2.7 lb. in weight. A variety of common Rudd known as the golden Rudd is quite popular with pond keepers.

## *Rudd:*

35

*Gymnocephalus cernuus*

*Ruffe:*

This species resembles a small perch, however they only grow to around 4 to 6 inches long and tend to be olive brown to golden brown along its back with a yellowish white underbelly.

The dorsal fin protrudes proudly just like that of the perch, the dorsal is made up from sharp spines and care should be taken when handling this small fish. Note the two dorsal fins are actually fused in to one, these small fish have been caught just over 5 oz. in weight.

Although this is a quite small species, it has been recorded up to 10 inches in length, the Ruffe is a very aggressive fish for its size. Feeds on small aquatic bugs and larvae, however these small fish will take a worm bait.

### *Gasterosteus aculaeatus*

The Stickleback is probably the first small fish caught by many school children. It is a small, streamlined, torpedo shaped fish, with a broad tail fin. This fish has the presence of two to four, but typically three, sharp spines on the back in front of the dorsal fin. The sides of this stickleback are usually covered with large bony plates. The back of the fish is dark grey, greyish or bluish green, and the flanks are silvery. During the spawning season, males develop a metallic sheen and a prominent bright orange or red colouration on the front part of the under side. Most populations are anadromous, they live in seawater but breed in fresh or brackish water and are very tolerant of changes in salinity, due to this fact this species is a subject of great interest to physiologists. Sticklebacks are easy to catch and keep in an aquarium, line caught up to 4 drams in weight.

**3-spined**          **Stickleback:**

*Barbatula barbatula*

*Stone loach:*

Stone loach are a long, slender shaped fish with three pairs of barbules around their under slung mouth. The back and flanks have black mottling over a dark olive brown colouration, blending to a narrow greyish white under belly. The dorsal and caudal fins are rounded off with their tips slightly notched, these are made up from fin rays and not spines.

They are small fish with an average length of just 8 to 10cm. Their superb camouflage does not assist easy location in the shallows as this species prefer to hide under rocks or other debris, great patience will be needed to spot them.

These fish can grow to 8 drams in weight. These fish sometimes venture into estuaries but not into brackish water. They live on the bottom often partly buried, the stone loach are particularly active at night when they stir up the sand and gravel looking for the small invertebrates on which they feed.

### *Tinca tinca*

Usually olive or tawny green in colour with shade variations from dark to light, a specifically bred golden colour also exists. The body shape of this species is very similar to the carp and although not always very clear to see, Tench have two small barbels, one each side of the mouth. Males have larger ventral fins than females, and in both, the fins are very thick and fleshy. Tench have bright orange eyes and also very small scales and skin slimy to the touch, it is always best to handle this and any other fish with a damp towel, never touch this species with dry hands as this will damage the fish. Tench reach maturity after about two years they have a nocturnal habit feeding on the bottom in the habitat in which they live, stirring up mud in the process. These have been caught over 15 lbs. in the United kingdom, however this species can reach over 25lbs.

**Tench:**

*Tinca tinca*

## Golden Tench:

An artificially bred variety called the golden Tench or Schlei is a popular ornamental fish for ponds, however these are also now found in some lakes and rivers.

This form varies in colour from pale gold through to red, and some fish have black or red spots on the flanks and fins. There is no record weight for this fish as they are classed as the same species as the standard Tench.

Larger Tench may be found in gravel pits or deep, slow moving water with a clay or silt bottom and large amounts of aquatic vegetation.

The best methods and bait to catch Tench are float fishing and ledgering with a swim feeder using maggots, sweet corn, bread, and worms, fish weighting over 2 lb. can be very strong fighters when caught on a rod and reel.

### *Sander lucioperca*

Also known as the Pikeperch, the body is elongate and the nose is pointed, there are numerous small teeth in the jaws and several large fangs in front, these are very sharp and can cause nasty injuries, great care must be taken around this area of the fish as with the Pike, another species with nasty teeth. There are two dorsal fins, the first spiny and separated by a narrow interspace from the second. The anal fin has 2 to 3 spines and 11 to 13 soft rays, the pelvic fins are widely spaced.

The lateral line has an average of 90 scales in it. Colouration is greenish grey or brown on the back and sides becoming lighter on the lower sides and white on the belly. Juvenile fish have 8 to 10 indistinct dusky bars on the sides, these are faint in the adult. The dorsal and tail fins tend to be dark spotted.

**Zander:**

41

### *Game fish introduction:*

All of the fish species on the following pages are classed as game fish, the majority of which are caught on fly fishing tackle or netted in certain circumstances. Please note fishing for this category of fish species requires a separate license to the Environment Agency rod fishing licence used for catching coarse water species, also there are numerous rules that must be adhered to on particular waters when game fishing, for instance many venues only allow an angler to take a set number of fish, with all others being returned to the water, others have banned the use of live baits like worms for instance. If you are ever to fish a new venue and you are unsure of the rules and regulations it is always better to ask a member of staff or if you can find one a local angler or tackle dealer. Heavy fines and confiscation of fishing equipment can be the norm and legally, unfortunately for the angler, they are in the right, it is better to be in the know, than to end up in court for poaching!

**Dorsal fin**

**Pectoral fin**

**Pelvic fin**

**Anal fin**

**Adipose**

**Caudal fin**

## Salmon and Trout:

Apart from the Trout, Charr and Powan that are found in some lakes and small streams around the United Kingdom, the majority of Salmon and Trout are migratory as they are born in fresh water, live in the sea and return to fresh water to spawn.

*Salvelinus alpinus*

*Artic Charr:*

The Artic Charr is closely related to both salmon and trout and has many characteristics of both including that it can be found in fresh and saltwater. Like all chars, Arctic char have light coloured spots on a dark background. They are variable in colour depending on environmental conditions within their lake of residence and time of year.

The back is dark with a brownish or olive tint, the sides are lighter, fading to a pale belly. The overall colour may be brown, yellow, gold, orange, or red. As the char approaches spawning, the spots, belly, and fins take on a bright orange, red, or gold cast, and the lower fins have brilliant white leading edges. The entire body may become golden or orange. Spawning colours are more exaggerated in males than in females. This species can grow in excess of 10 lbs.

*Coregonus lavaretus*

There are approximately only nine landlocked groups of this species in the United kingdom. These fish were thought to be in serious decline, however recent studies show that Powan populations are relatively healthy and recent declines in numbers were put down to the introduction of Ruffe an invasive species shown earlier in the book, which tend to eat the Powan eggs and fry.

Thanks to such initiatives as conservation in Loch Lomond  for the species by release of hundreds of Powan this species should be around in the United Kingdom for many years to come.

Although similar fish are found around England and wales the Scottish Powan is a distinct species. Colouration is a silver grey with darker fins and in some cases a whitish silver with silver grey fins.

*Powan:*

***Thymallus thymallus***

## Grayling:

Grayling are a species of the salmon family, and is found mainly in rivers. It is readily distinguished from other members of the Salmon family by the large dorsal fin and quite large scales. Colouration is often silvery or grey in colour, however mature fish can be darker, particularly the males around spawning time. Caught up to and over 4 lbs. with a record weight of 6.7 kg (15 lb.) world wide.

The grayling is distinguished from other members of its family by the presence of a number of dorsal and anal spines, between 5 and 8 dorsal and 3 to 4 anal, the remainder of the rays in these fins are softer rays. Grayling are an omnivorous species, they will literally eat anything in the range of small fish fry, insects, crustaceans and even aquatic vegetation as long as it is in cold, clean, running riverine waters. These can be fished for throughout the coarse fishing season.

### *Salmo salar*

The body of the Atlantic salmon is elongate but does become deeper with age. Jaws in adult males become greatly hooked just before and during breeding. The dorsal fin is quite short and has a small  adipose fin behind it, the pelvic fins are in line with the base below latter half of dorsal fin.

The anal fin is around the same size as the dorsal and the caudal fin is fairly deeply forked. The scales of the fish are small, with approximately 140 in the lateral line.

Colouration is brown, or green blue across the back, the flanks are silvery and belly is white. Above the lateral line black spots can be found. This species has been caught up to 64 lbs. Atlantic salmon that do not journey to sea, usually because of past human interference, are known as land locked salmon.

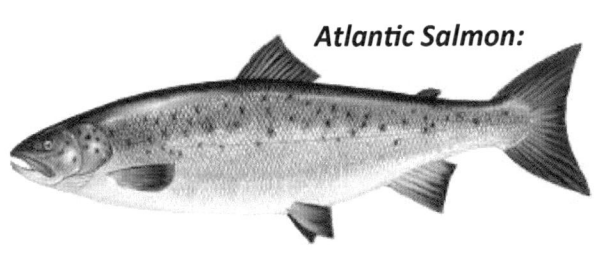

**Atlantic Salmon:**

*Orcorhynchus gorbuscha*

*Pacific Salmon:*

As with all salmon, in addition to the dorsal fin they also have an adipose fin. The fish is characterized by a white mouth with black gums, no teeth on the tongue. During their spawning the male develops a pronounced humped back.

Colouration is a bright silver, after spawning their colouring changes to pale grey on the back with yellowish white. Pacific salmon average 4.8 pounds in weight. Typically, salmon are anadromous, they are born in fresh water, migrate to the ocean, then return to fresh water to reproduce, however, populations of several species are restricted to fresh water through their lives, these are known as land locked. Folklore has it that the fish return back to the exact spot where they were born to spawn, however, it is known that some fish do enter the wrong fresh water system be it a stream, river or estuary.

48

### *Salvelinus fontinalis*

The American brook trout has a green to brown basic colouration with a distinctive marbled pattern of lighter shades across the flanks and back and extending at least to the dorsal fin, and often to the tail. There is a distinctive sprinkling of red dots, surrounded by blue haloes along the flanks of the fish, whilst the belly and lower fins are reddish in colour, the latter with white leading edges. Often the belly, particularly of the males, becomes very red or orange when the fish are spawning. These fish have been Caught up to 8lbs in weight. A hybrid between the brook trout and the brown trout known as the tiger trout can be found in parts of the United kingdom, but this is quite rare and almost always with the intervention of people, this does naturally occur around the world but fry are usually sterile.

### *American brook Trout:*

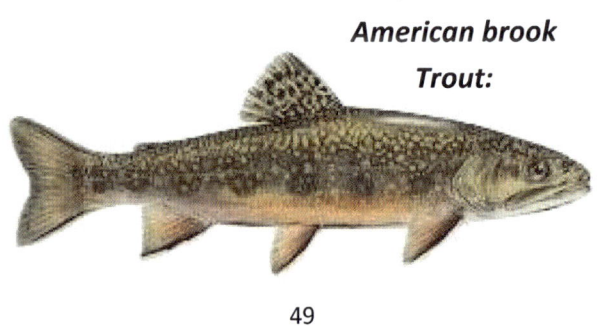

49

*Salmo trutta*

**Brown Trout:**

Brown Trout are found throughout England, Scotland, Wales and Ireland in both running and still waters. Brown trout are typically streamlined, highly spotted fishes, with brown background colouration varying to yellow, and with black, orange, or red spots. Natural brown trout grow up to and over 31 lbs. however, genetically enhanced fish can grow much larger thanks to the growth hormones mixed in with their diet, this can be quite common in the States but tends to happen less in the U.K. Brown trout were introduced into the wild in Australia from stocks in the United kingdom, eggs were taken from the river Itchen and survived a four month voyage from Cornwall to Melbourne on a sailing ship named Norfolk and by 1866 more than 170 young brown trout were swimming around a river hatchery in Tasmania, a true testament to a hardy fish species.

### *Oncorhynchus mykiss*

Rainbow trout also called redband trout, were originally introduced from North America this species has found favour with anglers thanks to it's fast growth rate and less stringent requirements for high water quality than the native brown trout. Rainbow trout are beautiful looking fish, with colouring and patterns that vary widely depending on habitat, age, and spawning condition. They have a torpedo shaped body and are generally bluish green or yellowy green in colour with a pink streak along their sides, the underbelly is a bright white but can sometimes be quite dusky, and small black spots on their back and fins. A number of fisheries specialise in growing very large rainbow trout, a twenty pound fish is now quite common, however the heaviest recorded fish stands at a whopping 36lb 14oz 8 drams, truly a monster of a fish, there is currently no recorded wild fish weight.

## *Rainbow Trout:*

*Salmo trutta*

*Sea Trout:*

Sea trout are the sea going version of the brown trout, only returning to fresh water to spawn, this fish is known by many different names around the U.K. including, Sewin, Finnock, Peal, Mort and white trout. The appearance of the adult fish changes as spawning approaches, Sea trout entering the river in spring and early summer are inevitably bright silver, with black spots, after a few weeks in the river their appearance starts to change. The silver becoming dull the females typically fade to grey almost a pewter or lead shade sometimes with a purple or dull brown tint, males frequently develop a pinkish sheen and eventually a deep reddish brown colouration. The existing spots become more prominent and new spots may develop, often to the extent that the back and flanks of the fish are entirely covered. Natural sea trout can weigh up to and over 28 lbs.

### Cray fish: introduction

An armour plated alien invading menace is eating its way through the wildlife in Britain's waterways the formidable American **Signal Cray fish** poses a massive threat to the native species in rivers, lakes and ponds. On the surface everything might appear fairly normal, beneath the surface of the water the crayfish is waging war on anything that stands in its way.

The six inch long killing machine has already annihilated the smaller native **White Claw Cray fish** from most of the waterways in the south of England. As a voracious predator it will eat almost anything it finds including plants, invertebrates, snails, small fish and fish eggs, what's more it's also a cannibal that often makes a meal of its own young.

The **Signal Cray fish** also digs burrows up to three feet long in river banks where each year it lays in excess of 250 eggs at a time, during a time of increased flooding the numbers and size of the burrows, is increasingly causing river banks to collapse, particularly in southern chalk streams.

Introduced in the 1970s and bred on farms for the

restaurant trade a handful of escapee's have now grown to an aquatic army numbering millions these have infiltrated river systems from Cornwall to Scotland.

The *Signal Cray fish* is extremely aggressive, encased in a tough shell and armed with two large pincers. They are equally at home on land and can walk for several miles across country in search of new territory.

When the crayfish move into a stretch of river it is virtually a death warrant for other species.

The loss of plants means there are fewer places for insect larvae and for fish to lay their eggs which in some rivers has reduced trout and salmon stocks. The invasive crayfish has now reached plague proportions and marine biologists have been desperately seeking a way of halting its relentless spread. Suggestions have included breeding huge numbers of sterile males, the same that happens with mosquito control, to wreck breeding success rates.

Trapping and taking the *Signal Cray fish* out of the water would have to be done on a massive scale to have any significant impact and attempts to introduce a specific crayfish fatal disease has also failed.

### *Here are a few Signal Cray fish facts:*

The female breeds from the age of about two when it is 40mm long. She breeds once a year and averages 275 eggs. The eggs are fertilised by the male during October and November.

They are carried by the female folded within her tail until May when the young are released - if they can escape her jaws. The Signal is bigger and more aggressive than native crayfish. They are less fussy in what they eat and more successful and rapidly colonise new areas.

The Signal carries a fungus which is fatal to native crayfish, and the Signal \crayfish can live up to 12 years.

Note the more detailed main claw colouration.

### *Signal Cray fish*

### *White clawed crayfish:*

(Austropotamobius pallipes) lives in a wide variety of

clean aquatic habitats but tend to favour hard water streams and rivers.

A major threat to our native **white clawed crayfish** is posed by introductions of a non native species of crayfish, which have been farmed in England since the late 1970s.

Soon after this a virulent disease caused by the fungus Aphanomyces astaci broke out and spread rapidly causing drastic losses of native crayfish in rivers around England. It is firmly believed that this disease was introduced and is spread by the most frequently farmed species, the **North American signal crayfish** (Pacifastacus leniusculus), a carrier of the disease.

Crayfish plague can be introduced into a body of water, not only by entry of **signal crayfish** but also by water, fish or equipment that has been in contact with signals, this greatly increases the risk to remaining ***white clawed crayfish*** populations. Signal and other non-native crayfish are larger and more aggressive than the native species and are able to produce more young, consequently, the introduced species pose a threat not only because many are disease carriers, but also through predation and competition with white clawed crayfish. In Britain, signal crayfish are now very well established in the wild. In Northern Ireland no crayfish farms have been established and crayfish plague is unknown, although it occurs in the Republic of Ireland.

It is only in areas free of disease that ***white clawed Cray fish*** are likely to survive in the future. In many areas of the united kingdom the ***white clawed Cray fish*** are a protected species, this should be a matter of law as our native Cray fish is fast becoming an endangered species, so should you come across one of these small feisty white claws, help it on its way, however, should you stumble across an alien invading signal Cray fish, that's different, these do make a very nice meal and lets face it, it's wrong to waste food!!!!!!!!

***Cooked <u>Signal Cray fish</u> with a slice of lemon tastes great!***

Printed in Great Britain
by Amazon